Baroque Music
For
TRUMPET
with Piano Accompaniment

Edited and Arranged by
ROBERT NAGEL

T0050664

CONTENTS

Foreword

There is a great wealth of baroque music for the trumpet. However, much of it has been inaccessible to the young trumpet student. Most of this repertoire requires either string orchestra with continuo, or singers or woodwind instruments, which create problems of performance for the student. Much of this music is still not published in readily available editions. Furthermore, the relatively high tessitura of most baroque trumpet parts causes endurance and range difficulties for the student.

This collection of representative trumpet works written by the great masters of the baroque has been realized, transposed and adapted specifically for the musical enrichment of the literature for trumpet and piano available to the aspiring young performer.

In conjunction with this collection, Robert Nagel has recorded all of the compositions herein, with piano accompaniment, on Mentor Music Record Album LP-101*. While the well-known artist performs on one side of the album, the record also includes a complete piano part alone, so that the young performer may play along with the recording, if he so wishes.

Robert Nagel's musical career began at the age of eight. He studied trumpet with Dr. Frank Simon, renowned Sousa Band soloist, and Earnest Williams, well-known symphony and solo trumpeter. Nagel holds B.S. and M.S. degrees from Juilliard School of Music.

He teaches trumpet, horn and trombone at the Yale University School of Music, and is a member of the artist-faculty of the Aspen Music Festival and Music School. In addition, he is the founder and director of the New York Brass Quintet, a pioneer group, presenting brass chamber music to young audiences.

The Publishers

*Mentor Music Record Album LP-101 is available from your music dealer or Mentor Music, 17 Broadview Rd., Brookfield, Conn. 06804

ARIA*

from *Cantata No. 77*

JOHANN SEBASTIAN BACH
(1685 - 1750)
arranged by Robert Nagel

Original Key

B♭ Trumpet (*8va below original*)

ritard. second time only

* Original for Alto Voice, Trumpet and Continuo.

B♭ Trumpet

ALLEGRO
from *Concerto for Trumpet and Strings*
(First Movement)

GIUSEPPE TORELLI
(1658 - 1709)
arranged by Robert Nagel

Original Key: D

B♭ Trumpet

SONATA DETTA DEL NERO*

from *Modo per imparare a sonare di Tromba (1638)*

Original Key: C

GIROLAMO FANTINI
(1600-?)
arranged by Robert Nagel

B♭ Trumpet

* Original for Solo Trumpet and Continuo.

MARCHE GAY*

from *Symphonies for the King's Bed Chamber*

JEAN-BAPTISTE LULLY
(1632 - 1687)
arranged by Robert Nagel

Original Key: D

Bb Trumpet

* Original for Trumpet, Winds, Strings and Timpani.

ANGLAISE, MINUET AND HORNPIPE

from *Suite for Trumpet, 2 Oboes and Strings*

GEORGE FREDERICK HANDEL
(1685 - 1759)
arranged by Robert Nagel

Original Key: D

Bb Trumpet

I ANGLAISE

ARIA*

from *Cantata No. 77*

JOHANN SEBASTIAN BACH
(1685 - 1750)
arranged by Robert Nagel

Original Key

* Original for Alto Voice, Trumpet and Continuo.

4

D.S. 𝄋 al Fine

D.S. 𝄋 al Fine

ALLEGRO

from *Concerto for Trumpet and Strings*

(First Movement)

GIUSEPPE TORELLI
(1658-1709)
arranged by Robert Nagel

Original Key: D

SONATA DETTA DEL NERO*

from *Modo per imparare a sonare di Tromba (1688)*

GIROLAMO FANTINI
(1600-?)
arranged by Robert Nagel

Original Key: C

*Original for Solo Trumpet and Continuo.

Allegretto (♩ = c. 116)

MARCHE GAY*

from *Symphonies for the King's Bed Chamber*

JEAN-BAPTISTE LULLY
(1632 - 1687)
arranged by Robert Nagel

Original Key: D

* Original for Trumpet, Winds, Strings and Timpani.

Ⓒ

Ⓓ

ANGLAISE, MINUET AND HORNPIPE

from *Suite for Trumpet, 2 Oboes and Strings*

GEORGE FREDERICK HANDEL
(1685 - 1759)
arranged by Robert Nagel

Original Key: D

I ANGLAISE

II MINUET

III HORNPIPE

ARIA*

from *Cantata No. 43*

JOHANN SEBASTIAN BACH
(1685 - 1750)
arranged by Robert Nagel

Original Key

* Original for Bass Voice, Trumpet and Continuo.

Ⓒ

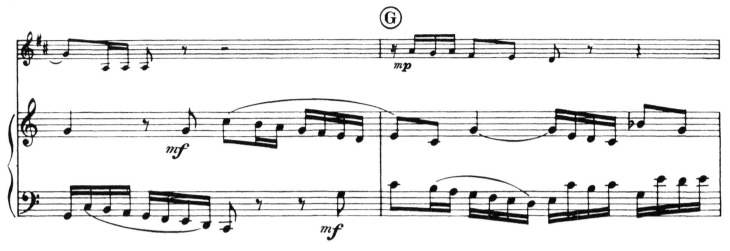

TWO PIECES*

from *Heroic Music*

G. P. TELEMANN
(1681-1767)

arranged by Robert Nagel

Original Key

I

Bb Trumpet

Piano
(Keyboard)

* Original for Violin, Flute or other melody instrument and continuo.

II

Allegro

TRUMPET TUNE*

from *Dioclesian, Act IV*

HENRY PURCELL
(1659–1695)
arranged by Robert Nagel

Original Key: D

Allegro maestoso

Bb Trumpets

Piano
(Keyboard)

(in absence of 2nd Trumpet)

* Original for two Trumpets and Continuo.

TRUMPET AIR*

from *The Indian Queen*

HENRY PURCELL
(1659 - 1695)
arranged by Robert Nagel

Original Key: C

* Original for Solo Trumpet and Strings.

THE TRUMPET SHALL SOUND*

(abridged)

from *The Messiah*

GEORGE FREDERICK HANDEL
(1685 - 1759)

arranged by Robert Nagel

Original Key: D

* Original for Bass Voice, Trumpet and Strings.

SONATA CON TROMBA*

(Fifth Movement)

ARCANGELO CORELLI
(1653 - 1713)
arranged by Robert Nagel

Original Key: D

* Original for Trumpet and Strings.
Used by permission of Mentor Music, Inc.

II MINUET

III HORNPIPE

ARIA*

from *Cantata No. 43*

Original Key

B♭ Trumpet *(8va below original)*

JOHANN SEBASTIAN BACH
(1685 - 1750)
arranged by Robert Nagel

*Original for Bass Voice, Trumpet and Continuo.

TWO PIECES*

from *Heroic Music*

Original Key

G. P. TELEMANN
(1681-1767)

arranged by Robert Nagel

B♭ Trumpet

* Original for Violin, Flute or other melody instrument and Continuo.

TRUMPET TUNE*

from *Dioclesian, Act IV*

HENRY PURCELL
(1659 - 1695)

arranged by Robert Nagel

Original Key: D

Bb Trumpets

Allegro maestoso

* Original for two Trumpets and Continuo.

TRUMPET AIR*

from *The Indian Queen*

Original Key: C

HENRY PURCELL
(1659 - 1695)
arranged by Robert Nagel

Bb Trumpet

* Original for Solo Trumpet and Strings.

THE TRUMPET SHALL SOUND*

(abridged)

from *The Messiah*

GEORGE FREDERICK HANDEL
(1685 - 1759)
arranged by Robert Nagel

Original Key: D

Bb Trumpet

* Original for Bass Voice, Solo Trumpet and Strings.

SONATA CON TROMBA*

(Fifth Movement)

ARCANGELO CORELLI
(1653 - 1713)
arranged by Robert Nagel

Original Key: D

B♭ Trumpet

* Original for Solo Trumpet and Strings.
Used by permission of Mentor Music, Inc.